FASTEST WOMAN ON EARTH

FASTEST WOMAN
ON EARTH

Alida Thacher

Illustrated by Ken Bachaus

RAINTREE PUBLISHERS
Milwaukee • Toronto • Melbourne • London

Copyright © 1980, Raintree Publishers Inc.

All rights reserved. No part of this book may be reproduced or utilized in any form or by any means, electronic or mechanical, including photocopying, recording, or by any information storage and retrieval system, without permission in writing from the Publisher. Inquiries should be addressed to Raintree Publishers Inc., 205 West Highland Avenue, Milwaukee, Wisconsin 53203.

Library of Congress Number: 79-21047

1 2 3 4 5 6 7 8 9 0 84 83 82 81 80

Printed and bound in the United States of America.

Library of Congress Cataloging in Publication Data

Thacher, Alida M.
    Fastest woman on earth.

    SUMMARY: Traces the death-defying career of Kitty O'Neil, a drag racer, stunt woman, and the holder of land speed records.
    1. O'Neil, Kitty — Juvenile Literature.
2. Automobile racing drivers — United States — Biography — Juvenile literature. 3. Stunt men and women — United States — Biography — Juvenile literature.
[1. O'Neil, Kitty. 2. Automobile racing drivers.
3. Stunt men and women] I. Bachaus, Ken.
II. Title.
GV1032.T48A33   796.7'2'0924   [B]   [92]   79-21047
ISBN 0-8172-1566-2 lib. bdg.

CONTENTS

CHAPTER 1

Faster Than Anyone...Almost

The day was December 4, 1976. The place was a desert in the state of Oregon. Kitty O'Neil, a very special person, was about to try a very special thing. She aimed to break some speed records in the *Motivator*, which was a land vehicle that looked like a missile.

First, Kitty O'Neil planned to top Lee Breedlove's eleven-year-old record of 308 mph. This would give her the women's land speed record. After that, she wanted to break Gary Gabelich's record of 623 mph. That would make her the fastest human being on land. Once she had done these things, there was one more speed she planned to beat: 740 mph, the speed of sound.

You might guess that Kitty O'Neil is an ambitious person. And, when it comes to working toward her goals, nothing stops her—not being a woman in a man's sport, and not being totally deaf since she was a baby. If anything, things like these only make Kitty fight harder for her dreams.

The *Motivator* was pretty special itself. It was more a rocket than a car. It was thirty-eight feet long and made of fiberglass and aluminum. It had only three wheels. The *Motivator's* engine was huge. It worked like a rocket. One hundred gallons were needed to get the *Motivator* up to 600 mph.

One thing the *Motivator* had going for it was its size. It was smaller and lighter than most of its kind. And its seat was so small that Kitty had to squeeze into it, even though she is not big and weighs less than 100 pounds.

There were two dangers in Kitty driving the *Motivator* at such high speeds. Because it did not weigh much, it could become airborne. That is, it might take off into the air. The other danger was that Kitty could black out because of the high speed. But Kitty didn't seem the least bit worried.

The eleven-mile track on the desert seemed perfect. It was far away from everything. The surface was hard and smooth.

Nearby mountains protected the track from wind. It seemed a fine place to try for a speed record.

On December 4, everyone got to work.

According to the rules, Kitty had to make two runs. First she would go up the course. Then she would make a return run. The runs had to be made within two hours of each other. The weather and driving conditions would then be about the same. The speeds of the runs were then put together, and the average speed became the official time.

Kitty squeezed into the tiny seat. It was shaped so that she was almost lying on her back. Because she was deaf, she could not talk to her team by

radio. Instead, they made hand signals to her. Three, two, one, zero, and she was off—whizzing like a bullet down the course. At the end of that run, helpers checked all the *Motivator*'s systems to make sure everything was in order. Then, they turned the *Motivator* around. Kitty crawled back into the seat. She raced back to the starting point on her second run. Average time: 322 mph. Her first goal had been met. Kitty had just broken the women's land speed record.

Kitty was pleased with the feel of the *Motivator*. She said, "The car was handling beautifully. I wanted to go faster."

And so she did. Two days later, on her ninth and tenth runs, Kitty's official time was 512.083 mph. At one point she was clocked going 618.3 mph—only 4 mph under the world's record. Going that speed, it took her five miles to stop—even with the help of three drag parachutes.

The team was ready to go for all of it the next day. Kitty was very pleased. "It's just beautiful," she said. "Everything looks like I'm going through water. I don't want to stop. I want to drive forever. God is with me."

Bill Frederick, who thought up the *Motivator*, agreed with Kitty. "Tomorrow," he said, "we shove the men out of the way."

But it was not to be. And it was for reasons

having nothing to do with either the *Motivator* or Kitty O'Neil.

Duffy Hambleton, Kitty's husband, had paid $100,000 for Kitty to have the chance to break the women's land speed record in the *Motivator*. A Chicago toy maker had paid $25,000 for a man named Hal Needham to try for the men's record in the machine. The first week in December, Needham could not make it. He sent word that Kitty should try for the men's record instead. The toy maker, however, didn't want it that way. He said that Needham—and no one else—could go for the men's record. And he had the right to say so.

Everybody was angry, but nobody could do a thing about it. Duffy Hambleton said, "They just won't let a woman hold the world speed record. They think it would make men look bad. They just won't let this little ninety-five-pound girl be the first to beat a man's world speed record.

"She's been deaf since she was four months old. She has fought off illnesses. She is the best able to drive this car to a new world land speed record—and they won't let her just because she is a woman."

Kitty was crushed. She was used to problems, but this was too much.

"It's the only thing I wanted to do," she said. "I want to break the world's record. But they don't want me to. They want a man to break the world's record.

"And I got hurt.

"But I'm not going to give up. I'm going to fight. It's just like being deaf. To overcome a handicap, you've got to fight. Like a challenge to conquer. That's what it's all about."

That's Kitty O'Neil for you—a fighter and a winner all the way.

CHAPTER 2

A World of Silence

Kitty was born in 1946 in Corpus Christi, Texas. She was a healthy baby. But at the age of four months, she came down with three different diseases at once —measles, mumps, and chicken pox. She lived through them, but paid a price. Kitty lost all her hearing.

There are two things, it seems, that Kitty got from her mother Patsy. The first is the strong straight looks of a Cherokee Indian. The second is the determination to succeed no matter what.

Being deaf in a hearing world is very hard, as any deaf person can tell you. But Patsy wanted her daughter to overcome her handicap and do great things with her life.

So Patsy and Kitty moved to Wichita Falls, Texas. Patsy went to college there. She wanted to learn how to teach Kitty. She wanted to help her bridge the gap between her deafness and the world outside. Patsy became so interested in

teaching deaf children that she later opened the School for Listening Eyes in Wichita Falls.

Patsy also taught Kitty other things. For example, Kitty learned to swim while she was still a baby.

Another thing Patsy taught Kitty was how to follow directions. Kitty could not hear directions, so she learned to watch for them with her eyes. She understood them through her mother's touch. From very early on, Kitty began to develop great powers of concentration.

Next, Patsy began to teach her daughter to communicate with the hearing world. Kitty remembers, "My mom never wanted me to learn sign language. She wanted me to talk to other people like hearing people." And so Kitty never learned signing, talking with her hands. Instead, she was drilled on reading lips and sounding out words that she herself could not hear. One way that Kitty would learn to speak was to feel her mother's throat sounding out different words. Then, Kitty would try to match the sounds.

Kitty learned these difficult skills very well. She reads lips and speaks with ease. It is hard to believe that she's deaf. She's so easy to understand that, at first, it appears that she has only a slight speech problem.

Kitty could communicate very well by the time she was eight. So she began public school in the third grade.

Think of how hard it would be to be deaf in a classroom of hearing people. There would be so many things you could not easily understand. It would be hard to follow the directions your teacher gave to the class. It would be hard to take part in things. So many times, you'd need to ask questions, and asking questions can be so hard. It means calling attention to yourself. You can feel like you're wasting other people's time. If you're deaf and you don't speak the way everyone else does, these problems can become even worse.

If someone spoke in class while Kitty wasn't looking at his or her lips, she wouldn't know what had been said. She had to watch closely to see where others were looking and what gestures they were making so she could follow what was happening.

And Kitty could not hear the whispered secrets in the classroom or the shouts and calls on the playground. Making friends is hard when you're deaf.

But both Kitty and her mother were determined that she would succeed in school. She worked hard through each grade, and she got good marks all the way.

Kitty O'Neil. She was a very special person from the beginning. She was doing all sorts of things deaf people weren't supposed to be able to do. She even learned to play musical instruments

while she was young. With her mother's help, Kitty began studying the piano and the cello. She couldn't hear the tones she made, but she could use her other senses to play. With the piano, she used her eyes and her sense of rhythm. For the cello, she used her sense of touch. She could feel the movements of the strings, and their tiny changes. In that way, she kept the notes on pitch.

A lot of growing up for Kitty was plain hard work, but there was one area that gave her real joy from the beginning—sports. From the time she had first started to swim as a baby, she had always liked sports. When she was twelve years

old, she began to win races, not just for fun. Her best race was the 100-meter freestyle. She began taking part in races all over Texas, as well as in some other states.

Diving also interested Kitty. She wanted to learn to dive, but no one would help her. Everyone worried that because she was deaf, she wouldn't be able to keep her balance. And one must have good balance to dive.

But those people didn't know that Kitty does what she puts her mind to.

One day, at a swimming meet in Oklahoma, everyone found out about that, though. Kitty remembers, "One of our team's divers didn't show up. I hardly knew one dive from another, but I asked them to let me try."

And at that meet, she won first place and re-ceived a gold medal in diving. It was a real thrill for her to see everyone cheering for her.

"It was my first real medal," she says. "So I gave up swimming races right then to work only on diving."

Kitty O'Neil had had her first taste of winning. And it was a taste too sweet to forget.

CHAPTER
3

That Sweet Success

When Kitty decides to do something, she thinks only of that. And that's just what she did with diving. She worked long hours. She practiced dives over and over. And, as is so often the case, her hard work paid off.

Only six months after that day at the Oklahoma meet, she took top honors at the Amateur Athletic Union (AAU) Southwest District Junior Olympics. Kitty O'Neil—diving champion. That had a nice ring to it.

Because of that win, a story about Kitty appeared in the *New York Times Magazine* in August 1961. One person who read the story was Dr. Sammy Lee, a two-time Olympic diving champion.

After he stopped diving, Lee had started his own school for teaching diving. He worked with young people he thought might become champions.

When he read about Kitty, he thought she was championship material. He talked to Kitty and her mother about his school. Working with Lee would mean moving from Texas to Anaheim, California, where the school was. But both Kitty and her mother felt the move would be worth it.

So, when Kitty was sixteen, the two of them packed their bags and moved west. Kitty had to work hard. She attended Anaheim High School in the mornings. In the afternoon she went to diving school for four hours of practice. Evenings and weekends she caught up with her homework.

Kitty was both a three-meter and a platform diver. She worked on diving boards at levels up to ten meters (about thirty-three feet). From that height, her body could sometimes reach speeds of forty mph by the time she reached the water.

Because Kitty was deaf, she had to be taught in a different way. She could not hear shouted directions about when to turn or twist in the dives. So instead, Lee used a gun loaded with blanks to tell her. She could feel the vibrations the blanks made in the air. That way she would know when to change her positions.

Kitty's great powers of concentration helped her learn her dives. "After a couple of tries with a very hard dive," Lee said, "she would know what to do. From then on she could actually 'feel' her way through it." After that, it was just a matter of practicing.

Kitty did make mistakes, of course, and painful ones at that. Landing in the water the wrong way at such high speeds could really hurt. But Kitty didn't let that slow her down. She was, as usual, determined to do what she had set out to do.

Her determination carried her through in other parts of her life, too. Life was not always easy for her. She was turned down for jobs because of her deafness. She knew she could do the work, but no one trusted that. At moments like that, her mother helped her to remain determined never to give up.

Kitty's hard work paid off for her in high school. She graduated with honors from Anaheim High School in 1963. And that, along with the fifteen gold medals and five trophies she had earned in diving, brought her another honor. She was named "Young American of the Month" by *American Youth Magazine*.

After graduation, Kitty continued to work on her diving. She won the women's ten-meter diving event in the AAU Nationals. This made her a national champion.

But Kitty had plans to become an international champion. She had a very special goal in mind. She was getting ready for the 1964 Olympics in Tokyo, Japan.

Again, she would be in the ten-meter diving event. But first she had to win a place on the United States team.

During one of her trial meets, Kitty hurt herself. On one of the dives, she did not lock her thumbs together tightly enough. Instead of punching the water cleanly with her fists, her hands broke away from each other. The force pushed one hand toward her face. Her wrist hit her forehead, and her wrist was broken.

This would put a halt to almost any usual person's dreams about the Olympics. But it couldn't

stop Kitty. In spite of the accident, she made the team. At her first time in the Olympics, she finished in eighth place.

And both she and coach Lee knew she could win the gold medal in the 1968 Mexico City Olympics. They had four years to train for it.

But tragedy again struck Kitty O'Neil's life. She came down with spinal meningitis, a deadly disease.

Many people die of the disease. But that was not what the doctors thought would happen to Kitty. Instead, they thought she would be paralyzed for life, unable to move.

But—it almost seems usual for her—Kitty came back again. She regained full use of her body, though not in time to put in the months of work needed to win an Olympic gold medal.

Her illness marked the end of diving for Kitty. During those years, she had won a total of thirty-eight blue ribbons, seventeen first place trophies, and thirty-one gold medals.

Now it was time for her to try new things.

CHAPTER 4

Danger, Thrills, and Chills

At the age of eighteen, Kitty said, "I can do anything. I like to do things people say I can't do because I'm deaf. I have to work harder than some, but look at the fun I have proving they're wrong."

And anything was just about what Kitty began trying next—anything, that is, that had to do with danger and speed. She began racing just about everything she could lay her hands on. She didn't stick to sports cars, top-fuel dragsters, and motorcycles. She was also racing things like speedboats, snowmobiles, and dune buggies. And she always went as fast as they could take her, no matter what might happen to her. "I love to go fast, and I love danger," she says.

Then she adds, "I'm really crazy."

When she wasn't racing machines, she enjoyed other kinds of daring sports—skydiving, hang gliding, scuba diving, and karate. She explored

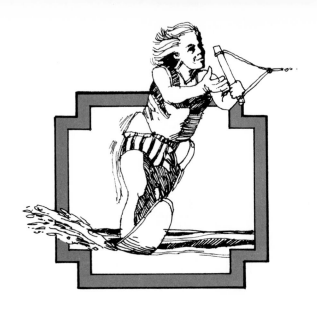

excitement by land, air, and water. She always looked for that bigger thrill.

In 1970, she began doing a little water skiing. But of course, Kitty couldn't be satisfied with a nice easy trip around a lake. Instead, she went for a speed record. And that year she water skied at 104.85 mph. This was faster than any woman had ever water-skied before.

At one time or another, Kitty has held twenty-two records, and that list is likely to keep growing. Kitty can't seem to stop pushing everything as hard as she can.

"I guess I like danger and thrills," she says. "But mostly I want always to have a goal, some dream that I can try for."

While she was going after her records, sometimes she raced only with herself, and sometimes she raced against others.

She liked drag racing. This sport was started in

order to stop teenagers from racing each other up and down city streets in cars. Instead, they were given a track to race on. The idea of drag racing is to see how fast you can get your car to go over a half-mile track. The best car for this race is called a dragster. Its weight is on the rear wheels, and this helps it get up speed quickly. A good dragster and a good driver can reach speeds of more than 200 mph in as little as 7 seconds. No wonder Kitty liked the sport!

She also raced off-road automobiles and dune

buggies. She raced against Indianapolis 500 winner Parnelli Jones and driver Mickey Thompson. Thompson held many national and international records. Like Kitty, Thompson also tried and failed to break the world land speed record.

Cross-country motorcycle racing also seemed exciting to Kitty. Racing dirt bikes means that your mind has to work a hundred feet ahead of your body. You must watch for changes in the ground, and for rocks. You must be doing this while your body is working with the bike, keeping it going fast without tipping it over. You must concentrate hard.

Kitty studied this sport for awhile. Then she began racing. A short time after she had started dirt biking, she had earned an expert rating from the American Motorcycle Association.

But staying in one country was not Kitty's style. Soon, she was the only woman to hold a license from the Federation Internationale Motorcycliste, known as the FIM. This group passes on world records. The FIM had clocked Kitty's land speed in the *Motivator*. With a license from FIM, she could race in international motorcycle events.

She took part in long-distance dirt bike races in Mexico—like the Mint 400, the Baja 500, and the Mexican 1,000. Again, she raced against some of the best racers in the world. One champion was

Malcolm Smith, who is probably the best known cross-country motorcycle racer anywhere.

Racing in other countries is exciting, but for Kitty, it presents a problem. It is nearly impossible for her to communicate. Not surprisingly, she lip reads only English. Kitty's speech is easy to understand for people who know English well, but not for others. As a deaf person, Kitty can feel alone at home in America. But in other countries, this feeling becomes greater. It's just about impossible for her to travel without someone who can talk for her. And Kitty, who is so used to doing whatever she wants with no help from anyone, doesn't like this.

One day in 1972, when Kitty was at a motorcycle rally in Saddleback, California, she got to talking with one of the other racers. He was Duffy Hambleton, who had once worked in a bank. When Kitty met him, he was the owner of World Wide Enterprises, a company that sold certain things to movie companies.

Hambleton was amazed at Kitty O'Neil. "She was unbelievable," he remembers. "I couldn't imagine being able to drive a motorcycle the way she could without hearing what gear the bike was in or knowing when someone was coming up behind her."

She liked him, too. Within the year, they were

married. Although they are now divorced, Duffy played an important part in Kitty's life.

At first, Kitty tried living married life as a housewife. She and Duffy lived on a large ranch in Fillmore, California, surrounded by orange trees. Duffy had both a teenage son and daughter, and Kitty put a lot of work and spirit into her new role of stepmother. She taught them things she had learned. She helped them try for their dreams and to think like winners—the way she did.

She spent part of her days keeping in shape. Every morning she would run eight to ten miles. After that, she would work out with light weights. She continues this fitness program today.

Still, life was awfully tame for her, a person who liked danger and thrills. And so she began looking for new dreams and new goals.

CHAPTER 5

Fall Girl

Besides running World Wide Enterprises, Kitty's husband Duffy had been working in Hollywood as a stuntman for many years. He was a member of Stunts Unlimited, which performed most of the stunt work in movies and television.

Kitty was finding her own job as a housewife a little too calm and quiet. And watching Duffy make his living by danger made her want to do that too.

As Duffy remembers, "Kitty was getting restless, so I asked her what she'd like to do. She said, 'Well, why don't I just do what you do? Teach me how to do stunts.'

"She'd been coming to our practice sessions, and she already knew a lot about the business. So we began teaching her how to fall and fake a fight and roll a car and so on."

Some of the things weren't really new to Kitty. She'd rolled her first car when she was sixteen. It wasn't her car, however. It was her mother's favorite!

Kitty worked with Stunts Unlimited for two years. She learned to do many stunts. She also learned some of the more dangerous ones.

Duffy said, "When she began doing all of it, she really razzled and dazzled them. I mean, I thought I knew what she could do, but she went far beyond that. We would only have to explain something once, and she'd do it. She has great powers of concentration."

Those powers of concentration are the same powers that helped her learn lip reading and speech, the same powers that helped her feel her dives right after only a couple of tries, and that helped her drive dirt bikes and speedboats as fast as they could go.

In 1976, Kitty got her Screen Actors Guild card. Now she could show everyone how good she was at stunts.

Her first job was doing stunt work on the television show *The Bionic Woman*. It was a program filled with action and adventure, and lots of stunt work. One of Kitty's tasks was to race the bionic woman in a dune buggy across the sand. Kitty was supposed to lose. Suddenly, at a very high speed, Kitty's dune buggy spun out of control— or at least that's how it appeared on the TV set. Kitty and the dune buggy rolled over and over and exploded into flames. But it was all in a day's work for a stunt woman.

Loren James, who has worked in movies for more than twenty years, thinks highly of Kitty's work. "She has developed in six months to a point that usually requires two to three years. She is very calm, cool, and collected under pressure."

Some people call that quality concentration.

Again and again, Kitty proved she had no fear and that she was willing to try just about any stunt she was asked to do. For one film she was working on, she fell 105 feet from a cliff into a river—the highest fall ever done on film by a woman. Since then, she has made several more dives and falls of more than 100 feet, one of the highest being 127 feet.

Falls were certainly not the only high-risk stunts Kitty tried. She was the first woman ever to perform a "cannon roll"—a car roll-over that is triggered by a special explosive device instead of by the driver. That's a stunt she has done often.

She was also the first woman ever to do a complete "fire gag"—a stunt that's anything but funny. Kitty was dressed in a protective suit and given a tube to breathe through. Then, she was

covered with glue and set on fire. Although the protective suit could prevent her from being burned, it couldn't keep her from becoming very hot. In fact, the suit became sort of an oven. Between the time that Kitty was set on fire and the time the cameras had shot enough film for the scene, the inside of her suit had reached 200 degrees! When the crew had put the flames out, Kitty came out of the suit sweaty, but smiling.

Kitty never thinks that she can't do something just because she's a woman, any more than she thinks she can't do something because she's deaf.

Her long string of stunts led to another "First Woman Ever" accomplishment. All thirty-one male members of Stunts Unlimited voted Kitty in as the group's first female member. Duffy said, "That was quite an accomplishment, considering that when you talk about a stunt men's organization, you're talking about people who think much of themselves as men."

But Stunts Unlimited was beginning to change in 1974. Shortly after Kitty joined, the group took in another stunt woman, Janet Brady.

Stunt work is still Kitty's basic bread and butter. She has worked in many movies and television shows.

She'll do anything, from falling off tall buildings to getting knocked around in fist fights to being put in water in a flooding aircraft carrier. There is little that is quiet or easy about making a living by stunt work.

Although her record has not been free from accidents, most of the time she comes out of her stunts feeling great and ready to do more. "I never get scared," she says. "Think positive. If you get scared, you get hurt." And Kitty firmly believes that, with the help of God, she can accomplish anything.

CHAPTER 6

Crashing the Sound Barrier

"Deaf people can be number one," says Kitty O'Neil, and she has proved that. It is a lesson she wants others—both deaf people and others—to know.

In some ways, Kitty fits more easily among people who hear well than among deaf people. She bought a hearing aid when she was thirty. Now she can hear some things. She has no trouble talking with most people who can hear. But she needs help when talking with deaf people who use sign language.

But Kitty cares about others who are deaf. She knows firsthand that even when a deaf person does great things, there will still be people who won't understand. There will be those who treat a deaf person as though he or she is stupid or helpless. There will be those who think that just because a person can't hear, he or she also cannot have feelings about things.

"I'd like to spend more time with deaf people—because it's safer," she told a group of deaf school children. Safe from the cruelty and insensitivities of the hearing world. Safe from the hearing world's ideas about what deaf people can and can't do.

Kitty is a special deaf person in many ways. Few people—deaf or hearing—have her great drive to do things. Her concentration and her great purpose are astounding.

"Think positive," she tells deaf people. "Never

look back, and never give up." That is how Kitty has become the person she is today. She refuses to be discouraged anytime.

And so Kitty herself is an inspiration. She is an inspiration to deaf people, who might be told they can't do something because they don't hear. She is an inspiration to women, who might be told they can't do certain things because they aren't men. And she is an inspiration to people with illnesses, who might be told they can't come back to their former strength.

People are beginning to know more about Kitty and what she has done. In 1979, she was given an award by the Alexander Graham Bell Association. She was chosen as the person who has done the most to help the handicapped in the United States.

A toy company is making Kitty O'Neil dolls now. A TV movie was made about her life. Kitty, however, wasn't pleased with the film. She didn't think the movie presented the truth.

Kitty knows what to do about this. She wants to write a book about her life. Then, she wants to make a movie based on the book. This time, she will have a lot to say about how the movie is made. And, she wants to play herself in the movie. There's no doubt that when this movie gets made, it will be a lot different from the first one.

There's one thing Kitty knows she wants in her movie. She wants it to have captions and sign language. She wants the film to be a success story about a deaf person that other *deaf* people can understand and enjoy.

And so Kitty continues to dream and to make goals for herself. She plans to open a couple of schools. She wants one school to teach sports to handicapped people. She wants others to have the joy she has known through sports.

Her other school would be to develop what she calls "one world communication." Because of her trouble communicating in other countries, she wants to find a way for people around the world to understand each other's language.

And Kitty still has a few goals for herself in the area of danger and thrills—like making a power boat jump of 200 feet to set a new world's record.

And she hasn't forgotten the dream of going faster than 740 mph on land. Perhaps the biggest and best goal of all for this special deaf person is to travel faster than the speed of sound.

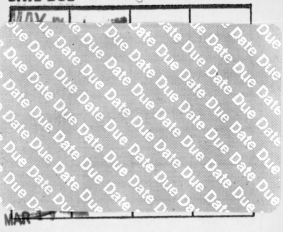